Ten Years Gone

2nd Edition

By

Michael "Sals" Guisao

<u>Dedication</u>

First I'd like to dedicate this to my family: Los Guisao's. Los Cruz's, Los Sepulveda's, Los Arenas's, Los Del Rios's, Los Melendez's.

My best friend Cutler for always believing in me.

My brothers Willy, Juan, and JJ for always encouraging me.

My parents William and Eugenia, thank you for always believing in me, and having nothing but confidence in my abilities.

Alex for suggesting that I should do a book with all my poems.

Victoria for always being encouraging and supportive.

Special shout out to

my brothers in The Kliq.

Alejandra (Nena)

Alondra

Amanda

Andres

Brayan

Manny (El Jucrem)

Alejandro (El Primo)

Jessie Messie

Kajuana

Karina

Roger

Roca

To Liam C, Silly Lilly, Aaron William Hilario, Arianna Jade, Baby Nati, Coda, Aria, and Liam L, y'all can do anything. So get out there and do it. Fuck fear, fuck self-doubt. Do not hold yourself back.

"I was never insane except upon occasions when my heart was touched."

-Edgar Allan Poe

La Danza De Nencatacoa y Huitaca

Bochica, the Chief of the Andes gods, wandered the mountains sad, alone, and bored from his own marriage. One night, he noticed a star shining brighter than the moon. So he reached up and plucked the star from the night sky, like fruit from a tree.

The star burned brighter and warmer than anything Bochica had ever witnessed before. So he dropped the star into a lake. Nearby, Nencatacoa wandered around the mountains, drunk on chicha, a drink of fermented corn and pineapple. Dressed in gold, he loved poetry, art, and music. In a drunken stupor, he sang to the midnight sky. He noticed the star falling and watched it landing in the lake nearby.

The water extinguished the flames of the star, and a being emerged from it. This being was Goddess Huitaca, who swam to the land. She was beautiful, voluptuous, desirable, and hypnotic. Her smile was as beautiful as the full moon.

After setting foot on land, the owls came and dried her with gusts of air from their many wings. The snakes slithered by and begged to dance with her. Nencatacoa, in stunned amazement, fell to the ground and passed out in a drunken stupor. As he slept, he dreamed of her beauty.

The next day, Nencatacoa awoke and went searching for Huitaca. She was with the other gods, and Bochica was teaching her about the land and of the Muisca people who worshipped them. The chief of the Gods was falling madly in love with Huitaca. Sadly, to his dismay, she had no interest in romantic relationships; she only cared for music and drinking.

Nencatacoa volunteered to show Huitaca around the land. He introduced her to the many animals, such as the foxes and bears, that followed him around. He showed her the many flowers, which she loved. He taught her the names of the insects, such as the butterflies.

At night, they would visit the Muisca people. They ate fruits and meat. They drank chicha and laughed, as the people sang and danced. The music of the Muisca people moved Huitaca deeply, causing her to writhe and dance. Her dancing caused the owls to hoot, and the rattle snakes to shake their rattlers to the music.

As she danced the night away, Nencatacoa was inspired to paint. He painted a mural on the wall of a bohio, a circular house with clay walls and a straw roof. He painted the image of Huitaca covered in flowers, dancing with the snakes and owls.

When Nencatacoa was done, he searched for Huitaca. She had left to make love to some of the Muisca men and women. This broke his heart. Instead of acting in hate, he left to wander the forest and sing songs of love and admiration for Huitaca's beauty. His songs were so beautifully painful that the foxes and bears joined him in singing.

Soon, the news of what had transpired came to Bochica. Bochica was jealous of Nencatacoa's love for Huitaca and was furious at his own inability to take Huitaca as his wife. So, he cast a spell and turned Huitaca into an owl.

Nencatacoa was enraged by this but was powerless to do anything against his chief. From that night forth, you could always find Nencatacoa drunk on chicha, singing songs of love to Huitaca the owl, hoping that one day Bochica will find it in his heart to turn her back to a being.

<u>For Huitaca</u>

Imagine when the sun first kissed the rose.

Imagine when the wolf first howled at the moon.

That is your effect my sweet goddess Huitaca.

That is the feeling you inspire into me.

You are my greatest sin.

You are my sweetest confession.

I am the moth dancing close to your warm flames.

I am the priest that worships your sweet name.

You are both my addiction and my affliction.

You are the north star shining brightly throughout space
and time.

__Mad Love__

I wish to bury the memories of your remains.

To stop fighting with the ghost of your memory

To put out the fury that lingers within me still.

I want to feel peace and tranquility.

To let go and move on

I feel haunted like a grave.

Wanting to feel your sweet embrace.

Like a flower whose thorns poisons me

Like a remedy to soothe me

Hollow and empty, waiting to be filled.

I hate thee so and love thee still.

Like a thief in the night, you stole my heart.

Like the bane of my existence, you tore me apart.

The more I gave the less I got back.

For every sonnet written, for every song sung.

Your venomous tongue scorned and cursed me like a plague.

You reminded me of my worthlessness.

You reminded me that I'm undeserving.

You treated me how everyone mistreats you.

For every abuse taken

Your wrath saw only me.

Why couldn't you loved me, like I love you?

Catalyst

I've hated this world.

I've loathed living in it.

I've made enemies.

I've drawn lines and boundaries.

I've begged for death.

I've waited for the god damn end…

Then there was you.

A fire erupted in the ice box known as my heart.

The sun rose like a phoenix over the dark winter of my life.

The feeling is immense.

The feeling is overwhelming.

Lesson of One

In all my years and all my schooling,

I've learned a thousand rules and read a thousand books.

I've learned a thousand lessons.

But the one lesson I couldn't be taught,

The one lesson I could never understand,

Was of one woman and one man.

What is love? What is devotion?

It sounds like nonsense and rubbish.

There's no way it exists.

But I finally learned.

I see it's true.

Love does exist.

I learned it from the first time we kissed.

Love is real.

Love is true.

For you love me and I love you.

What I want

I just want to feel alive.

To be filled with the fires of inspiration

To be driven

To look into the abyss and find my destination.

I want to be reminded.

To be taken back to a happier place in time

When I was yours and you were mine

I want to rewrite the past.

Correct the mistakes made.

I want to start all over again.

Get things right this time around.

You were my muse.

My heart

My fire

The very embodiment of my dreams desire

Like an angel tending to my pain

Pointing me in the right direction

I've lost my way.

I feel myself falling.

Wishing to hear your voice.

Wishing you would answer my calling.

I would

If I could look at you in another way, I would.

If I could think of you in another way, I would.

If I could fight the power, you hold over me I wouldn't.

If I could l hate you with all my heart I wouldn't.

The heart wants what it wants.

And the eyes long for what it needs.

To look you in the eyes and make you feel what I feel.

To make you smile

To hear you laugh

To simply hear your voice

If I could have you like I do in my dreams I would

If I could hold your hands like I do in my dreams I would

If I could muster the strength to tell you all that I feel I
would

Accidental

What are we but accidents?

Accidents of love, hate, lust, wrath….

Accidents cause by the sea of emotions that we all drown
in.

What does it all mean?

Is there destiny or fate?

What is the plan for us all if all that we are, are happy
accidents?

Can I be thankful for a gift I didn't ask for?

Can I give this gift to someone more deserving?

Can I return this life to the two that created it?

All our pain, all our suffering

Do we blame it on an accident?

If we succeed if we do something right.

Was it by accident?

Death Requiem

Picture dying on a bed of roses.

The only music you hear is the rustling.

Of leaves as the wind passes through

The trees like spirits caught between realms.

The wind is a cold love song,

and the sun is the beacon of heaven.

Calling her children home.

Every blade of grass like the arms of

The damned springing out from the grave,

A reminder that Hell is never too far behind.

What are we but sinful angels looking for peace and acceptance?

Bacchus

I don't want to think.

I don't want to feel.

I want to drown myself in the music of my soul.

I want to kick up my feet and dance.

Like the fool I am.

To wear my smile like a mask.

and give my devilish laughter to then world.

Pluto

Take me out of winter,

Out of the darkness,

And bring me into the sunlight.

Let me hear the ocean sing,

Sing its song of glory.

Bury me in white sands,

And let the birds of paradise lay me to rest.

Let Calypso wear her white dress,

With marigolds in her hair,

And reclaim me as her own.

Let her lips be the chalice that I drink from

Her arms entomb me.

To Bacchus

Let Bacchus have his drink,

Let him have his dance,

Let him have his laugh.

In fields of poppy and marigold,

Let him have his carnival.

His cardinal sins are lust, pride, greed, and gluttony.

In thunder clouds of hash and opium,

In a sea of Poseidon's court,

I still dream of Elysium.

Condemned to Hades,

Swimming and drowning in the River Styx.

I pray to Aphrodite to be reunited with my darling
Demeter.

<u>Midnight Hour</u>

Take a midnight ride through my mind,

Wave goodbye to the ghosts of my psyche.

Enjoy the euphoria coursing through my veins.

Release the chains, and free the beast from within.

If you be Abel, then call me Caine.

I'm running loose,

And singing round the midnight pyre.

Fall in love with the Midnight Queen.

Light her smoke and pour her a drink.

Moon shines bright on drunken smiles.

And the Devil's children dance in the shadows.

Embrace your madness and become the drug you consume.

Take a midnight ride through your mind.

Break down the walls of your reality.

Fly high in the nighttime sky.

Become a storm, wild and free as nature.

Make love to the world,

And enjoy the midnight ride.

Let your worries rest,

And be a creature of the night.

Intoxication

In the absinthe of life

I think of you.

And find myself wanting.

Desiring

Thirsting

To have you shine in my eyes.

Likes the stars in the midnight sky.

The moons euphoria is nothing compared.

To the delirium you cause in me.

Sweet Embrace

Let me lay in your arms so that,

You may enjoy the outline of my smile.

To feel the velvet of your skin,

And the warmth of your sweet embrace.

Let the whispered word of love,

Ring in my ears like the hymns of Heaven.

You are the sun,

To I the weed.

You are the sensation,

My reminder that I still draw breath of life.

The living dream,

Found beneath the comforts of bedsheets.

<u>Obsessed</u>

There's a face that you see in the dark,

Lips that you've never kissed but

Can always taste.

Her name haunts your every thought, like an obsession.

She's an addiction,

An itch that you cannot scratch.

She is the remedy to what ails you.

She is the solution to your insanity.

The angel deaf to your prayers.

She

As beautiful as she was.

She was a broken mirror.

Every time I looked at her,

I saw all that was wrong with me.

I saw the evil in me,

I saw the devil in me.

I saw nothing but my sins in her.

As stubborn and unbending as I am,

She had the power to bring me to my knees.

As verbal as I am,

She had the power to silence my demons.

Running Away

It's the same reoccurring night terror.

You tell yourself that you're going to fix it,

But you're stuck on a loop.

You stick your fears, your worries in a bottle,

And you run, run, run as fast as you can,

You run, run, run from the dream police chasing you,

Through space and time you run, you fall.

You get stuck, you get caught, and you make it worse,

The same night terror stuck on a loop.

Fool in Love

Lust for love,

My fantasy, and deepest desire,

Like April's Fool I walked blindly into the fire.

Without remorse I took a leap into the sun

Like Icarus.

A festival of blackbirds,

I drink from the goblet of laughter.

<u>Gemini</u>

Her hair was as red as the fire of the sun,

her skin was as soft as lilies in the spring.

She smelled as sweet as the nectar of flowers.

Her soul was as black as coal,

her heart was as cold as an iceberg.

Her black abysmal hair curled and slithered like the snaked
of the gorgon Medusa.

Her lips were as loving as the fly traps of Venus.

Her heart was as warm as a mother's love.

Her soul shines brighter than the stars in the nighttime sky.

Angel Rose

In the winter of life,

I found a rose.

Soft and sweet,

It hit me hard like a dream.

Sprouting wings,

She called for me.

Took me by the hand,

And took me to the sun.

She showed me fire,

And brought me to peace.

Angel Rose desire.

She is my love.

She is my night.

I cry out for her.

I'd die for her.

Break me to my knees,

I'm begging baby please.

You are Beautiful

You are beautiful.

From the day you were born,

Till the day you leave this earth.

Inside and out.

Mind and spirit.

To all my five senses,

The very thought of you is beautiful.

My deepest most secret dreams of you are beautiful.

To say your name is an act of falling in love.

You are beautiful.

My Everything, My All

My love for you is an addiction.

It gets me though my day,

And keeps me warm at night.

You are the sunlight that shines upon my universe.

You are the starlight that makes me dream.

You are the queen that rules my kingdom.

You are my heart that rules my life.

You are my one and only.

Down to the River

Going down to the river to pray.

I'm a sinner.

I'm no winner.

Lord have mercy.

Lord have pity.

Please watch over me.

Going down to the river to pray.

Lord watch over my soul.

Help me walk through the valley of the shadow of death.

Help me survive in the concrete jungle.

Going down to the river to pray.

All That I AM

All that I am is 'cause of your sweet love.

When I look into your eyes,

I see fire in your heart.

I just wanna hold you in my arms,

And love you for all my life.

Spellbound

You put a spell on me.

You used black magic voodoo to seduce me.

You called my name into your cauldron.

You called upon the spirits to entrap me.

You followed me with a crystal ball.

Poisoned me with an apple.

You put a spell on me.

Now I'm yours forever.

My eyes see only yours.

My hands can only feel yours.

My dreams are only of you.

My prayers beg for you.

You put a spell on me,

And stole my heart.

You put a spell on me,

And now I'm yours and you are mine.

The Drifter

Based on a family story.

No one from outside of Albania, here in Antioquia, just outside of Titiribí, is ever considered a stranger. Except for the drifter. Once, a drifter came through the main carretera [road]. He wasn't very tall. He was dark from sun exposure, half-starved, and dehydrated. His clothes were dirty and ripped. It seemed he had been walking for days. The dirt collected on his bare feet was a lighter shade of brown than his skin. His lips were dry and cracked, like salted earth. His eyes were black and red where the white should have been. His eyes and mouth were wide open— como un boracho, too drunk to know where he was or where he was going.

Mita always helped anyone in need. She worked as a midwife, having helped over half the families in town with child birth. They say no one was gentler or more loving toward babies than Mita. She also sewed clothes, cooked for those in need, gave religious council, and medical aid. She was the most self-sacrificing and caring woman, who was never too tired or too busy to suture wounds or relocate dislocated bones.

She was completely fearless, often intervening in violent altercations between random people in town. Once, she even stood in front of a man with a loaded gun, who was about to kill another man he had already beaten in a fight. She was armed with only a stick from a nearby tree, yelling, "*Covarde* [coward], can't you see he's had enough? You've won. You made your point *hombre macho* [macho man]. *Desgraciado* [Wretch]! There's no need to kill a man over a game of Remi." The would-be killer

31

thanked her for stopping him from making an unforgivable mistake.

As the drifter came nearer to her house, his knees weakened, and he collapsed to the floor. Mita ran inside the house and came back with water. By the time she got to him, he was on the floor, convulsing. She kneeled down beside him and lifted his head, to give him water.

"Drink, drink," she said as she tried comforting him.

Her son-in-law Luis and a neighbor came running to help her bring him inside. As the two men came out, she was alarmed by how warm the drifter's body was getting. Slowly, smoke seeped out of every pore on his body. She quickly let go of him and took a few steps back. "Stay back, don't get any closer!" she warned Luis and the neighbor. Standing at a safe distance, she made the sign of the cross and prayed as the fire shot out of the drifter's mouth and eyes.

In seconds, he was a ball of flames screaming in great agony. The fire died, and all that remained was ash and burn marks, in the middle of the Carretera, where the drifter was lain. Mita stood and stared at the burn marks trying to make sense of what had just happened. The neighbors were terrified and confused.

Mita composed herself and told the others, "Go back home, light candles on your windowsills, and pray to the Virgen Del Carmen." Unfortunately for Mita, she couldn't do anything else, so she continued with her day as if nothing had happened.

That night it rained; but as the night continued, the rain got heavier. Sophia, Mita's daughter and Luis's wife, lived a few houses away. She had heard from Luis about the incident.

"Madre, I heard everything that happened. Are you alright?"

Mita assured Sophia that everything was fine. "Nothing could have saved him. Hopefully, his suffering is over. It doesn't matter now."

"It does matter. What if something bad happened to you? What if you had caught fire?"

Mita fired back, "Then I would be dead too, and hopefully, my daughter would be praying for me by now."

Sophia stared at her mother, angry because she wouldn't take her concerns seriously. "You have to think about yourself first, Mama."

"I haven't thought of myself since I married your father, and I stopped thinking about him when I had you."

"I thought you stopped thinking about him when he started drinking."

"Of course, we had you because he started drinking, and that's when I stopped thinking about him and focused on raising my daughter."

Sophia's frustration grew, "Why are you so stubborn, Mama?"

"It runs in the family."

"I worry that after all the good things you do for others, one day you will need help, and no one will be there for you, Mama."

Mita smiled, "God will be there for me. He knows that great evil has the power to do good and is not doing so. Now, hurry home before the rain gets worse. I'm fine. Don't forget to light candles and pray."

Mita was a widow and lived alone. Her home, like many the homes in La Albania in Antioquia, Colombia, was small—one-storied with a typical roof made of wooden beams, straw, and terracotta roof tiles. She tried going on with her nightly sewing as usual, but as the rain was beating down on her roof, she felt a slight headache. She tried ignoring her headache but kept pricking her fingers by accident. There were blood droplets on the clothes she was fixing. She grew more and more frustrated with each prick. Normally, she was so skilled with a thread and needle, she could sew anything blindfolded.

The rain came beating down. It shook the roof with each heavy drop. Mita's migraine worsened. Lightning crashed down, sounding as if the world were cracking apart, startling her. Soon the light went out, and Mita began wandering around the house with a lit candle. As she ventured in the darkness, she began to feel as if she were being followed. Hot breath on the back of her neck and a cold chill ran down her spine as if something evil was slowly creeping behind her. She went to her bedroom and lit candles on the bedside table, which she had turned into an altar. On it was a wooden crucifix, a small statue of the Holy Trinity made of silver, the Virgin of Chiquinquirá in porcelain, a scapular of the Virgen del Carmen, and a picture of Jose Gregorio. As she began reading from her Bible, she could hear the rain dying out.

Soon it was silent, and she was relieved. She made the sign of the cross, and said, "Thank you Lord, for watching over me." She heard a loud thump in the living room as if someone had pounded a large and heavy fist against the adobe wall. She quickly went over to investigate with a lit candle in one hand, and her rosary beads in the other. When she arrived, nothing was wrong with the room. Nothing was broken, nothing was moved, and then, she noticed something by the window. Something was behind her window curtains. It looked as if a man was hiding in her curtains. She fearfully crept closer. Her heart was racing, but she had to find out who was behind the curtains.

As she slowly drew her hand closer to the curtains, she asked, "Who's there?" A chair tipped over, hitting the floor and scaring her. She was forced to turn around. As she looked around trying to spot the fallen the chair, she was immediately wrapped in the window curtains.

She screamed out, "Help, please God, help!"

Mita wrestled with the curtains. As she looked for any kind of opening with her hands, she could immediately feel a large person on the other side holding the curtains around her. She struggled for a moment; she fell to the floor and dragged the curtains with her. As she pulled off the curtains from around her head, she saw that she was alone.

She got off the floor, quickly rolled up the curtains, and placed it on the couch to be dealt with in the morning. She walked slowly in the dark, back to her bedroom. As she walked down the hallway, she could hear something following her from behind. Every time she turned around; she saw nothing.

She kept reminding herself, "It's all in my head, nothing is there. I am all alone. I have nothing to be afraid of."

From the corner of her eye, she saw her reflection off the few framed pictures that hung in the hallway. In the reflection, she saw a dark shadowy figure standing behind her. Whenever she looked directly into the glass reflection, it would disappear.

She kept reminding herself, "Nothing is there, I am all alone, there's nothing to be scared of."

She finally reached her bedroom. The candle from her bedside table and altar was still lit, so she found another candle and placed it on top of her dresser for more lighting. She opened the middle dresser. Mita bent over to pull out her nightgown to go to bed. As she stood right back up holding her nightgown, she saw in the mirror, above her dresser, the drifter on the other side of the room with a sinister smile on his face. Blood dripped from every orifice in his body. Mita stared into the mirror and screamed louder than she ever had in her life.

* * *

The next morning, Sophia came into the house to check on Mita. She worried more and more as she walked through the house. The torn curtains were on the floor. The furniture was in disarray. A strange odor came from the kitchen. There were insects crawling all over the refrigerator and even more insects flying out as Sophia opened the door. All the food in the refrigerator had rotted overnight.

All the picture frames in the hallway had the glass cracked or broken to pieces and shattered all over the hallway floor. When she reached the bedroom, she slowly pushed the door open, only to have it slammed shut in front of her. She began calling out her mother's name but was silenced by a heavy thud that shook the door and the walls around it. She leaned in against the door to hear any sounds from within the room. All she could hear was the heavy breathing and low growl of a large beastlike creature. She stood against the door trying to think of what to do, and immediately panicked and screamed when something inside the room huffed and hit the door, shaking the walls around it once more. She left the house screaming, calling out for Luis. Luis and Sophia came back to the house with three other men.

Luis urged Sophia, "Stay outside. We will take care of this."

As they slowly walked through the house, their hearts sank with fear as they saw the disorder. They passed through the swarm of flies from the kitchen and into the hallway. After seeing the broken glass and scratch marks all over, two of the men cowered and ran out of the house.

Sophia dropped to her knees on the front porch and cried hysterically. She tried to stop the two men as they ran for their lives. "Where are you going? What happened? Is my mother okay?" she begged to know of her mother's safety.

Inside the house, Luis and his oldest friend Fernando continued down the hallway to Mita's bedroom. As they got closer to the bedroom door, they could hear a large beast huffing, and stomping its foot on the floor like a bull readying to defend itself.

Fernando had never felt fear as he did then. "What the hell is in there, Luis?"

Luis responded, "I don't know."

Luis slowly gripped the doorknob and felt that it wouldn't budge. He then kicked the door with all his might and the door swung open. Luis and Fernando could see a large, black, shadowy, beastlike figure standing in the center of the room. The door immediately swung shut once more. They stood dumbfounded and terrified at the ghostly image that they had just seen.

Luis told Fernando, "Leave. She's my mother-in-law. I'll deal with whatever the hell that was."

Fernando refused, "No way, man; I'm not going anywhere without you and the old woman."

They ran, shoulders first, and tackled the door, only to have it shoved back and closed with great force. The two men pushed against the door with all their strength. They felt the door slowly heat up. Black smoke came out every time they managed to push the door open. The two men screamed in agony as the flesh on their arms burned against the hot door. Neither man would give up.

After a few minutes of battling the door, they finally pushed the door open. Both men fell into the room on the floor. The room cleared as the force of the door pushed back the smoke. As they slowly got back to their feet, all they could see were scratch marks burned into the walls of the room. Mita was on the floor, drenched in sweat. She cried hysterically, her rosary beads smoldering in her hands. She struggled to form words but ranted belligerently and unintelligently.

Luis and Fernando came rushing out of the house carrying Mita together. Sophia let out a heavy cry seeing her mother in this condition. "Oh my god, Mama. What happened to her?"

Luis quickly took charge. "Fernando, run like hell and get Father Julano. Sophia, stay with your mother while I go get some water."

Sophia held Mita in her arms and prayed while they waited for Fernando to come back with the town priest. Mita looked up at Sophia and listened to her prayers. She mumbled desperately but was unable to form words. Mita's right hand shook violently as she struggled to make the sign of the cross.

Luis came running out of a neighbor's house with water. Sophia took the water from Luis and gave it to Mita, who drank with incredible thirst.

Finally, Fernando arrived with Father Julano. The priest acted without hesitation. Father Julano instructed, "Luis," pointing at Mita, "hold her arms down with all your might." Father Julano dropped down to his knees and rubbed holy oil in the sign of the cross on Mita's forehead. Hot steam rose from Mita's head. The priest washed the top of Mita's head with holy water and began praying, while holding his cross against her forehead.

Mita cried in sheer agony, begging for death, "Make him stop! Make it stop! I can't take it no more!" while the priest continued praying. Luis and Sophia struggled to hold her down. Sophia cried helplessly for her mother.

Once again, the sky darkened, and the rain clouds gathered. It began to drizzle. In seconds, it began to rain down on the main carretera. The rain was blindingly heavy and sounded like a heavy drum roll against the asphalt. Luis yelled for Fernando, "Get Sophia out of the rain." Sophia resisted, but Fernando had no choice but to drag her by force. As Sophia cried out her mother's name, she saw a small, shadowy figure down the road. The drifter was just standing, smiling, and watching Luis and the priest try to save Mita. The drifter watched with an evil smile. Lightning struck down a tree, and then, he was gone. In the deafening sound of heavy rain, Mita's screams were silenced, and Father Julano had stopped praying. In seconds, the heavy rain died down into a light drizzle. The drizzle stopped, the rains clouds dispersed, and gave way to the sun.

Mita gasped and opened her eyes. She looked up at Luis and the priest and gave a sigh of relief. The priest stood up and called to Sophia, "Go to her. It is over." She rejoined her mother. Sophia kneeled beside her mother, grabbed Mita's hand, and held it to her chin, crying tears of joy. The priest prayed, but also advised, "I don't want anyone entering the house until I've had a chance to cleanse it of any evil dwelling inside." Luis and Fernando carried Mita back to Luis and Sophia's home so she could rest.

* * *

Later that night, the priest checked up on Mita. "How is she doing?"

Sophia with a smile of gratitude said, "She's rested and slowly eating sancocho de gallina [hen stew] and trying to regain her strength."

When asked about the event, Mita replied, "I don't know. It was like falling in and out of a really bad dream. Some things I remember, and some things, I don't want to remember."

The priest reassured everyone, and said, "Whatever happened inside Mita's home is best not remembered."

Luis looked down at the floor conflicted on whether to ask. Part of him didn't want to remember, but another part of him needed to know. "In Mita's room, I don't know what I saw, but I saw something." Sophia looked at Luis in fear of what she might hear. "It was big, huge. I don't know if it was man or beast."

Fernando added, "Yeah man, it was black. Like evil black. It looked at us with pure anger and hate."

Father Julano paused for a moment to gather his thoughts. "I wasn't there with you, so I cannot tell you what it was. The Devil can take many forms. He can either come as a man such as a drifter, an animal, or he can come as any of the twisted creatures of Hell."

At that moment Mita came out of the bedroom holding onto the walls. "Whatever it is, it's still in MY house."

"Mama, you should be in bed."

"Yes mija, in my bed, in my house."

"And if that thing is still in your house, what do you plan on doing?"

"What I always do inside my home. I will light a candle for the Virgin, pray to our Holy Father, and if I see that thing again, I will shove my candle far up its ..."

Father Julano stepped in between mother and daughter to comment, "I can go with you, and help cleanse the house of any evil spirits."

Sophia was angry with the priest for encouraging her mother. She turned to her husband Luis, in the hope of talking her mother out of going back home.

"I will go with them just to make sure it's safe to go inside the home."

Furious with Luis, Sophia retorted, "Are you seriously going to take my mother back there?"

Luis looked at the determination on Mita's face and looked at the anger in Sophia's eyes.

"I think I'm more afraid of your mother than whatever type of devil is inside that house."

"Fine, do whatever you want, Mama, you always do."

Sophia turned her back to the family. Mita walked up behind her daughter and hugged her. Sophia squeezed her mother's hands as she tried to fight back her tears.

"There's something evil inside your house, and I don't want it to take you away."

Mita smiled, "Great evil is having the power to do good and not doing so."

Luis led the way, armed with a machete. Father Julano carried his black leather bag, which contained holy water, incense, and a Bible. Mita followed her male protectors, holding her rosary beads tightly. Though a short walk, it left Mita out of breath. She had moments of dizziness.. The two men tried to talk her out of going home, but she insisted on continuing.

When they arrived, Mita was the first to reach for the door. A cold chill ran down the back of Father Julano's spine. A soft, cold wind blew in, and Luis turned around and looked out at the main carretera. While he was looking away, the front door swung open. Inside the house stood the large, black, shadowy beastlike figure. They stood petrified with fear. The creature reached for Mita, but Father Julano shoved Mita out of the way.

Father Julano gasped, "My God in Heaven!"

The black shadowy figure grabbed the priest, pulled him inside and slammed the door shut. Luis tried opening the door screaming, "Father Julano! Father!" The door wouldn't budge. Mita knew the door would not open. Luis kicked the door with all his might, but the door did not move an inch. He repeatedly slammed himself into the door, shoulder first. The door showed no signs of opening. Terrified and defeated, they listened to the sounds of the priest screaming in pain, followed by a loud noise of a large beast pounding its heavy fists against the floor. The house shook with each thud. Mita rushed toward the living room window, hoping to see what was going on, only to find the windows covered in blood splatter.

The priest stopped screaming, and Luis took a few steps back on to the main carretera. Mita cried while Luis stood terrified in silence, knowing that all hope was lost for the man of God.

In the shadowy distance, Luis saw a man walk down the road, a drifter. He wasn't very tall. He was dark from sun exposure, half-starved, and dehydrated. His clothes were dirty and ripped. It seemed he had been walking for days. The dirt collected on his bare feet was a lighter shade of brown than his skin. His lips were dry and cracked, like salted earth. His eyes were black, with red where the white should have been. His eyes and mouth were wide open—como un boracho, too drunk to remember where he was or where he was going. The drifter walked past Mita and Luis as if he couldn't see them. They said nothing, but as the drifter walked a little further down the road, they noticed the drifter looking back at them with a smile. He continued walking and eventually disappeared into the shadows.

Letting It Go

Have you ever stood above the clouds?

And stared at the Earth below.

The cold fresh air filling your lungs with

Each deep meditative inhalation.

To feel the weight of the world

Fall off your weary shoulders.

The freedom, the liberty,

Salvation through free fall.

To clear your mind, and close your rain flooded eyes,

And let fate be.

Have you ever let it all go and wipe the slate clean?

Let It Burn

Against the sorrow and the cold,

In the dying of the light.

In the darkness, at the end,

Find the last spark of life,

And let it burn!

Let it burn bright,

Let it ring in the chaos.

Be it anarchy, or order.

Let it ignite the soul,

And warm the chambers of the heart.

Flames of courage, hope, and inspire.

Let it burn,

Let it reign fire.

The Dark Lantern

Have you ever seen the black flame of a dark lantern?

It is the dark lantern of Charon.

The boatman of the dead.

Every eternal day and every infernal night,

He ferries the damn to Hades for two silver pieces.

His dark lantern is the light at the end of the tunnel.

His voice welcomes you after the suffering.

He is the hand reaching for yours at the end of it all.

When you feel forgotten and alone, he remembers the name
on your tombstone.

When you feel unloved, he places the black velvet of roses
on your grave.

Moth, Flies, and Spider Webs

I am the moth,

And you are the flame.

I lost my heart to you,

Now my life will never be the same.

With blood red lips,

Like roses on my grave.

I am the fly,

The prey to you,

My black widow mistress.

Let me dream,

Let me sleep in your loving web.

Let me die in your sweet chaotic embrace.

Lead Me Into Temptation

Midnight. The room was dark except for the little bit of moonlight that fell short of reaching the bed. Julano, naked in bed, tossed and turned. On his back, he woke up, and stared at the black void that was his ceiling. He sensed the silence and saw nothing. He knew. He felt that there was nothing and no one in his life. Julano was all alone.

There was a sound of something sliding from under his black, cotton bedsheet. Snakelike fingers slithered up his well-defined abs. His body quivered as he felt the rushing heat the moment her dark scarlet nails came down and rode the surface of his pecs. His inner thighs trembled with anticipation. He felt himself pulling back, but also felt himself needing to give in.

The bedsheet rose and hung from her head like a hood. From under the hood came a sinister smile. With that sinister smile appeared a face. Her dark, chocolate eyes hungered for its target. The nostrils flared and savored the aroma he was giving off. Her face drew closer and teased the surface of his cheek, as it ached to be touched. It was hot, it was electric, it was the feeling of being alive times ten.

Julano's body tightened and shook as soon as his pride was exposed to the welcoming warmth below her waist. His body felt like it was being drawn nearer and nearer to the edge of the earth. The fear and excitement were one combined feeling. Her legs pinned his down. It was like a gentle push closer. Her teeth thirsted for the taste of his lean and tout neck. His neck wanted to be penetrated by her teeth. Her whisper was smooth like pouring wine into a chalice, the sound echoed in his ear as she called to him, "Mon Cher."

He woke up abruptly.

Julano was drenched in sweat and his white bedsheets were stained with the juices of his dream. He got off the bed and walked in the dark, naked. His eyelids clenched the moment he turned on the light. Instinctually, he walked blindly, as his eyes adjusted to the light, toward the toilet in the bathroom, and reached for wet wipes to clean the bodily fluids off his manhood and stomach.

Julano walked back into his bedroom and grabbed the square tin container and the ashtray beside it. He went into the living room, sat down on the couch, and placed the ashtray on top of a book on demonology. His coffee table was littered in sketches of his dream mistress, post-it stickers, various books on the macabre, and Season 2 of Supernatural on DVD. He felt the tin container before opening it and retrieving a pre-rolled marijuana cone. Julano lit it and took a deep pull as he leaned into his couch. He exhaled a cloud of smoke as his right hand held the cone, and the left hand gently played with his nipple.

This midnight mistress had been haunting him for weeks. His girlfriend, Leonora, broke up with him as he couldn't explain the scratches and bite marks all over his body. Finding a loose strand of auburn hair in his bed was the last straw for her. As pleasurable as the nightly experience was, it was also pure agony. During the day, he hungered for more. It was all he could think of. Everywhere he went, he'd think of her. She was slowly becoming every woman in his sight. She was the coffee barista; she was the passenger in a nearby vehicle at the gas station; she was the librarian. Everywhere he went, he would see her image in other women. The smell of her auburn hair lingered in the very air he breathed. He felt her gaze watching his every move. It was hard to concentrate on anything as he would often hear her voice from a long distance, calling for him. It was an obsession he didn't want. It was an addiction he felt too weak to fight.

It was the beginning of October. He had to wait until the 20th for the next full moon. Until then, he had to gather his offerings. He already owned a king snake and a green tree python, which he cared for with love. Snakes were easy to purchase. Owls were harder to acquire. Purchasing an owl required permits. So, he had to capture one. Julano spent many nights lurking in Cold Spring Harbor State Park. He'd almost been caught by the authorities once or twice, but he finally captured a Great Horned Owl. Graveyard dirt from Oakland Cemetery, and white lilies were also easily acquired.

There's one misconception. Many ritual sacrifices were often conducted in the abandoned pump house, but the Walled Garden is where the magic needed to happen. Now that the full moon was ready to make an appearance, Julano would have to walk thirty minutes from his apartment on Pine Street to the Walled Garden in Untermeyer's Park. Both the pump house and the Walled Garden were located inside Untermeyer's.

The Walled Garden was designed to look like the Garden of Eden, as described in the Bible. The four man-made canals made a crossroad, which was exactly the location Julano needed. Five minutes to midnight, and Julano had his materials. He stripped naked. During the day, he was a fit and handsome young man, but in the darkness of the night, he was a shadowy wraith of his former self. The water in the four canals were still, almost solid looking, as if they were made of obsidian.

Julano stood in front of the fountain in the middle of the four canals, staring at the moon. He had his black

JanSport book bag next to him. From the bag, he first pulled out the green tree python, kissed her on the head, called her Lilith, and placed her on the stone border of the fountain. Second was the white and brown king snake, named Sammy, which he placed majestically opposite Lilith.

Next was a square tin can. He opened it to check the contents. Inside was the graveyard dirt from Oakland Cemetery, owl bones from the Great Horned Owl that he caught, lily petals, and a small, torn photo of himself. The photo was only half, the missing other half was of Leanora. He looked at the photo and remembered the romantic getaway to New Orleans. He quickly shut his eyes and shook his head to suppress the memory. With a small pocketknife from his bag, Julano slit his left palm and squeezed droplets of blood onto the graveyard dirt, owl bones, lily petals, and the torn photo.

He closed the tin can and tossed it into the center of the fountain. He pulled out another tin can, the tin can of pre-rolled marijuana cones. Also in it was a torn page from one of his books on demonology. He removed the last marijuana cone from the tin can, lit it, took a deep pull from it, and exhaled the smoke as he began to read the incantation.

"Annom lapos teykv eshgere Annom lapos tibykv hb'bereelym

absed anytib meykvl darelhtmsr lkpos

acciqh nu'avty me'eksh

tushlk usltm n'sepmtsh."

***

Now that it was said and done, he waited. Sammy and Lilith slithered about on the stone border of the fountain. Julano took another pull from his marijuana cone. His naked body quivered from the night cold. His sweaty hands trembled anxiously. His legs felt like crumbling columns, as his anticipation grew. His chest tightened as his breathing got deeper. Julano took another pull as the thought crept into his head that the ritual might not have worked.

Sammy and Lilith began to slither faster around the fountain. Julano noticed their strange behavior. He brought his hands over the fountain and felt heat coming from the black water. Coyotes in the area howled. Owls from all over landed in nearby trees, flapping their wings and hooting. Julano's body was on fire as his blood rushed all over and his heart raced.

The four plants that stuck out of the water in the fountain burst into flames. Two small feminine hands rose from under the black abyss of the fountain. She emerged divinely from the fountain and appeared to be levitating. Her nails were a dark shade of scarlet, her hair auburn, her eyes like chocolate, her lips a bright crimson, and her taut skin as pale as the moon. She took three steps and walked on the water toward Julano before inviting him into the fountain.

Without hesitation, Julano stepped onto the stone border of the fountain. Sammy and Lilith came to his sides and slithered halfway up his calves, almost encouraging him to step in. All the nocturnal creatures went silent with anticipation. Sammy and Lilith slid away as he took his first step in. The black water was a foot deep and made the skin on his lower legs red from the heat. Without taking his eyes off his prize, he took one last pull before throwing the marijuana cone away.

She spread her arms open wide and invited him closer. He felt helpless, but at the same time, comforted as he placed his face firmly between her warm, plump breasts. Her hands slithered from his shoulders down his back, clawing lines into his flesh. He was paralyzed with lust. He couldn't feel the burning of the hot, black water against his skin, nor the razor-hot sting of her nails. Blood dripped down the curves of his bare buttocks. His cock hardened as he slid his hands up her smooth back to embrace her. Warm tears filled his eyes as she kissed his forehead.

"Sh, sh, mon cher."

He looked up at her with joy. She smiled back at him. She tilted her head back as she pressed his head into her chest. The two of them fell into the fountain water. The splash of the water extinguished the flames of the burning water plants. The owls nearby scattered and flew from the trees. The coyotes howled one last howl as Sammy and Lilith slithered off the fountain and disappeared together into the night.

My Vow to You

With each passing day,

I love you all the more.

Like a thorn rose in love with the sun,

I need you like a sinner needs a prayer.

You are the elixir in my glass,

The melody ringing in my ears.

You are the end of my winter's past,

The light of dawn, my dream within a dream.

The high of my life, my perfect drug.

I was dead in the ground,

You filled my empty grave with life.

Missing Half

I am just a half,

An incompletion.

A sun without a moon,

Eternal infernal darkness without the light.

Lyrics without accompaniment.

I am the sorrow, to you the joy.

I found in you a spring of youth.

A bringer of smiles,

I'd walk endless miles to unlock the secrets of your
rewarding prize.

<u>Dead and Gone</u>

Dead and gone,

And moving on

The night is just as dark before the dawn.

Dead inside, dead and gone.

The Midnight Queen has left me,

Cold and alone like a broken shell of a dream.

She seduced with me with lies of a sweet dark eternity.

Abandoned me for her own farce of a fantasy.

The only place in this world for me is the cold sepulcher
confines of my mind.

In there I run and hide,

In there, I'm dead inside, dead and gone.

Luminescence

It was the first night home since Leonora had given birth to Baby Morgan. Leonora was relieved to be free from the three sleepless nights at St. Judith's Hospital. She was a light sleeper; always had been. The slightest sound or the dimmest source of light could disturb her slumber. Even the silently working overnight staff kept her stirring all through the nights.

Before becoming a new mother, Leonora took every precaution imaginable to ensure her eight hours of undisturbed rest. All electronics were either unplugged or hidden behind a cabinet door. A labyrinth of shades, curtains, and drapes to block out light from the nighttime moon or streetlamps. Now that she had a newborn in her life, she knew sleep would become a challenge. She refused her husband's suggestion of buying a baby monitor because she was confident that her child's cries would wake her up.

Edward, who was overseas with the military, had asked, "Are you sure you don't want a baby monitor?"

Leonora answered, "You know how sensitive I am to light. I won't be able to sleep. Besides, my mother took care of me without a baby monitor."

The baby's room was adjacent to the master bedroom. It was a pink and purple safe haven for Baby Morgan. Small patterns of butterflies and flowers decorated the walls. It was beautifully simple with old-fashioned baby dolls, made of soft fabric and stuffed with cotton. There were no electronic devices or toys that lit up with noises. The only exception was an antique music box that was handed down for generations, from mother to daughter.

Leonora's heart was filled with immeasurable joy when she laid Baby Morgan into her crib for the first time. She was a seven-pound bundle of angelic tranquility.

"Goodnight, my beautiful dreamer, queen of my song," said Leonora as she kissed her two fingers and gently pressed them on her child's forehead.

Before Leonora could leave the room, the music box began playing Beautiful Dreamer. She turned around and walked toward it, staring at it, trying to remember if the box was open or closed. In all the years she had the music box, it had never begun playing on its own without being wound. Afterward, Leonora turned off all the lights and went to bed. All was quiet in the house. All was peaceful. Not a single light shone for the exception of a small, white light emanating from Baby Morgan's room. The soft, dim glow reflected off the hardwood in the hallway outside the room, and crept its way into the master bedroom, awaking Leonora from her slumber.

She lifted her head up from the pillow and looked into the hallway but saw nothing. Leonora got up from her bed and went to check on Baby Morgan, who was still sound asleep and enjoying her infant dreams. She looked around the room in the dark. She saw nothing and went to bed.

Back in her bed and back to sleep. Leonora closed her eyes, relieved that her baby was home, safe, and asleep. There was nothing but silence in the air—a silence broken by the sighs of Baby Morgan.

Leonora's eyes shot open. She looked into the hallway and saw a soft white light coming from Baby Morgan's room. She sprung up from her bed and ran to her daughter's room. The light faded as soon as she hit the hallway. Leonora turned on the floor lamp near the crib and saw her baby's hazel eyes. The smile on Baby Morgan's face. She saw the mobile dancing above the crib. There was a faint fragrance in the air. It was sweet and soothing like her mother's Chantilly perfume, but she could not tell where it was coming from.

She inspected the room and found nothing alarming. So, she went back to bed, and back to sleep.

As she slept, she dreamed of being a child again. Her mother rocking her to sleep. She remembered her mother singing softly to the rhythm of the antique music box.

It had been so many years since her mother's passing that Leonora was overwhelmed by the memory she thought she had lost. Her eyes burned from the pain of her loss. A teardrop wrung out from her clenched eyelids and gently splashed on her pillow, waking her up from her dream.

She could see the soft glowing light from the hallway. She could hear the antique music box lull her daughter to sleep. She could smell the Chantilly perfume lingering in the air, the same as her mother once used. With a smile she whispered, "Mom, meet Morgan, your granddaughter. Goodnight to both my angels."

Pick Your Poison

There's a poison running through my veins,

and drugs running through my brain.

I lay here dying dreaming of your face,

and your angelic sweet embrace.

Beautiful Delusions

Her smile is the first ray of sunlight that I admire every
morning.

Her voice is like a hymn whenever she calls for me, her
warm embrace is my sanctuary.

Her lips are opiates.

She draws me in like a moth to a flame.

Nocte Regina

I love you.

Not for your body, not for your mind,
But for your soul.
Your soul was what made you shine.
Like a star in the nighttime sky.
Your spark ignited an inferno in my cold black heart.

Mi Negrita

Sol Negrita.
Te amo, te quiero.
Es me felizidad.
Mi bebidad.
Me traes tranquilidad.

Drunken Delirium

Drunken delirium
As I drift away
Staring at the midnight moon shine.
The stars in the sky couldn't match her witchcraft eyes.
Daughters of Hecate sing their songs of praise.
I drift away on nighttime clouds,
High above on Morpheus' magic.
The Midnight Queen dances in my dreams.

Requiem of a Dying Man

Sometimes I cannot see the sunshine,
In my twilight I fall on bloodied knees,
My prayer's tongue become an agonized scream.
My darling Persephone brings me black flowers and
whispered sonnets.
She is a spring of life,
A beautiful flower in bloom.
When all my angels fall,
I stand tall on the hanging gallows.
My brother Bacchus brings me joy from the chalice of
fools,
But even the finest wine can taste like the sorrow from the
river Styx.
A prince of the court of Olympus am I,
I often feel like Icarus,
Who dared to dream,
Only to fall.

I am

I am not perfect.

I am not always available.

I sometimes can't find my voice.

Or the words that needed to be said.

But I know what I want,

I know who I need in my life.

I know who I belong to.

I know who makes my heartbeat.

I don't know where I'm going.

I don't know what I'm doing.

Sometimes I need someone else to make my decisions for
me.

But I know where I need to be,

I know who to share my soul with,

I know the one decision I won't regret.

Her Liquor

If I could replace the shot glass for your succulent lips I
would.

Distilled fluids cannot compare to your divine nectar.

A sweet tender kiss from you can raise me high.

To dance on clouds like Icarus.

To fall for you like a fool caught in the April shower.

Moth to the Flame

God created moths to feed the flame.

A small flame compared to the sun,

Can still mean the world to the wind dancers.

Warmth and comfort to disguise the danger.

Where My Heart Is

A million days, a million miles,

My heart gazes over the mountains and across the sea.

Every lonely night I dream of my guiding star.

Every lonely night I dream of my midnight queen at the
end of my odyssey.

She's a beacon of light I pray would call me home.

Let my journey end where I belong,

Embraced in your arms.

Let me come home where my heart is.

El Guaro

I drink a water that burns like fire,

My soul's furnace is filled with the smoke of spent embers.

I dance to the song sung by blackbirds.

I dream of my Angel of Death,

She always ignores my prayers.

I count the days of my life.

On the scars of my body.

My face hides behind a mask.

Pearly white teeth hide my pain.

I am Icarus

My dream was to dance in the sunlight,

and bathe in its warm glory.

The ocean swallowed my broken body,

But my heart broke as I watched.

My burning desire fly away from my reach.

When I'm dead and gone,

Will the vultures enjoy the feast of my flesh?

Or laugh at the punchline of my descent?

Icarus the dreamer,

Icarus the fool in love with the sun.

Black Maiden

Have you ever seen the maiden?

In the long black dress,

With a little black bird.

She has the Devil in her eyes,

and an angel in her smile.

Defiant till The End

I laughed at each nail hammered into me.

I laughed at the hangman's noose wrapped around my
neck,

I laughed at the axe tickling my skin.

I laughed at the wooden stock imprisoning my body.

I am me.

Defiantly till the end,

Sinfully at the end,

Remorsefully at my end.

Praying for Pearly Gates,

Only seeing the brimstone and fire of my demise.

?

What good is the moon and all the stars in the midnight sky when they don't answer your prayers?

What good is the darkness when you have no love to hold you close?

What good is a whisper when your voice burns with rage?

Free and Numb

When I'm numb

It's like being dead and gone.

The song plays,

And the smile stains my face.

I can shake off my obligations,

I can erase away my titles,

And just be the man that God made.

I can break down the walls of insecurities,

And dance past the limits of morality.

If I fall my head will stand tall.

Despite hitting my lowest I still find myself at my highest.

At rock bottom I am numb and free.

Incomplete

I am just a half,

An incompletion.

A sun without a moon.

Eternal darkness without the light.

Lyrics without accompaniment.

I am the sorrow to you the joy.

I found in you a spring of youth.

A bringer of smiles,

I'd walk endless miles to unlock the secrets of your
treasured prize.

My Love for You

With each passing day
I love you all the more.
Like a rose in love with the sun,
I need you like a sinner needs a prayer.
You are the elixir in my shot glass,
The melody ringing in my ears.
You are the end of my winter's past,
The light of dawn, my dream within a dream.
The high of my life, my perfect beloved drug.
I was dead in the ground,
You filled my empty grave with life.

I, The Moth

I am the moth,
You are the flame.
I lost my heart to you,
Now my life will never be the same.
With red lips,

Like roses on my grave.

I am the fly,

The prey to you,

My black widow mistress.

Let me dream,

Let me sleep in your loving web.

Let me die,

In your sweet and final embrace.

<u>Midnight Queen</u>

Every firefly in the midnight sky,

Like guiding stars point to the midnight moon.

Every firefly in the midnight sky stands on ceremony for
the Midnight Queen.

The moon shines high to light up the spirit in their eyes.

Like Icarus I dream to fly to thee,

To touch thee,

And to hold thee.

Like a midnight fire I sing for thee.

Shots of Guaro

My little clear friend,

Bringer of the truth,

My mirror in a shot glass.

You force me to face myself,

You force me to stop and reflect upon the feelings I
desperately try to run away from.

Kingdoms comes, and kingdoms fall,

You're my friend through it all.

You peeled the smiling mask from off my skull.

Revealing the pain, I hid underneath it all.

Each distilled drop is a piece of my soul.

Stuck in a bottle and trying to crawl its way out.

A slow death that never comes,

A numbing pain flowing from a bottle.

Sedative meditation to bind me and blind me,

You're a silent song in my head to make me laugh.

You're a deadly poison dancing through my veins.

Fiery water running through my head,

Rebel yell till I'm dead.

Reflection in a Dream

I see you every time I look into the mirror.

You'll always be the only thing I like about myself.

I see you in every dream.

I see you in every thought I have.

You'll always be the better part of me.

What's good for the gander is good for the goose,

So by that definition

I only like myself when you like me,

but if you hate me than I have no choice but to hate myself.

Angel

I am an angel of the Lord.

he calls me Death,

but I am Mercy.

My white horse is weary,

but I keep riding on.

Black wings and a broke halo

my holy water burns its way out.

burns the tiny flask that contains it.

Call me a snake or servant,

but forever shall I be your man.

<u>We</u>

We run; we hide.

We believe our own lies.

We sing, we dance.

We become the empty mask.

we play our part.

Deception is our art.

With a smile and laugh

We hide our pain.

With a drink and a drug

We have our fun.

Avoiding truth of pain

We struggle through the day.

Upon this stage

We bleed.

We bury our rage.

Dead in My Head

If I could die tonight, I would,

If I could live tonight, I would,

The pendulum swings,

and I lay in my grave

in my coffin I sing

in my coffin I pray

six feet under I rejoice.

six feet under I enjoy.

Snowflakes on My Grave

It's cold outside, cold like me,

Cold like the winter solstice in my heart.

Snow covered flowers on the grave of the forgotten man.

The wind sings its lonely song to absent friends.

Crystalized tears dancing in the sky,

Frozen little flakes to fall and slumber on the

Cold stone baring my name.

I Lost My Laugh

I used to laugh, I used to feel my soul outcry in joy.

I had a laugh; it was the music of my heart could dance to.

I lived off my laughter, it healed all that wounds me.

If I could silence my rage, and laugh, and laugh, and laugh
I would.

The demons in my frown die each time I laugh.

If I could laugh just before the end,

There won't be a drop of rain to touch my grave.

Self-Loathing

I was thrown to the world.

Like a meat on the slab

The lamb to the slaughter

The Jew on the cross

Too smart to be taught.

Too tough to be beaten.

I'm sick of it all.

I'm sick of being me.

I hate myself and what I am.

I hate myself and ashamed that I am.

I should be grateful to be me.

Lucky of what I got.

I'm sick of my talents.

I'm fed up with my hell.

To serve my damned masters

Got nothing at all.

Not a scrap of a favor

I didn't get shit in return.

Fireflies

Fireflies blind my eyes.

Fireflies dancing in my mind

Like synapses kick starting my brain

Like psychotropic hallucinogens coursing through my veins

Fireflies call to me like spectral remnants of a dream.

Fireflies sing to me like the beauty of the midnight queen.

Pleasure of Pain

Chain me to the bed

And bring me to my knees

My midnight fantasy.

I live for you my euphoric dream.

Goddess of the night

My only prayer that gets me through the night

Sink your teeth through my flesh.

Make me bleed for your bliss.

Make me hurt for your wish.

My Demise

I found euphoria in a drink.

She was as beautiful as the sweetest dream.

My fantasy and deepest desire

She burned me like the moth in the fire.

Her name is my eulogy.

Her body was midnight pyre.

She was my dream within a dream.

My perfect drug

My sweet dark eternity

Drink Up

Drink until you're dumb.

Drink until you're two feet small.

Drink until you feel something.

Drunk until the pain goes away.

The liquid fire which brings you to the dance

Liquid courage to help you out of your zombie trance.

Pour in a glass, a shot, a red plastic cup.

Pour till you can laugh and enjoy the fuck up.

The Rock Bottom

Sometimes you hit the bottle,

Hit the rock,

Hit the bottom.

Sometimes all you see is darkness.

You can't see the light.

You can't win this fight.

You hear the dirt get thrown on the box.

You don't care no more,

You don't want to fight.

How long can you endure?

How much more shit can you take?

Little Miss Sunshine

She made the world beautiful with her soul.

She made the sun shine just for her.

In a world so dark and gray

She was the color that brightened up my day.

Flower Child

She's a sunflower grown in the winter snow.

She is the rose with the sharp pointy thorns.

She is the song that was written in the sky full of stars.

She is the night that carries the moon.

She is the high heard in the sound of laughter.

She is the wildfire burning inside my heart.

Stuck in My Head

I'm trapped in my mind.

Till the end of time

Far from my heart

She's a poem, she's a song, she's a work of art.

I don't want to think I just want to feel.

She's a lover's dream.

Dancing in a sunflower field

Pegasus

She is beautiful like a work of art.

She is addictive like a drug.

Her laughter is like music.

Her smile shines like the sun

It pains me not to tell her.

It tortures me not to hold her.

She's a Pegasus.

Free

Wild

Divine

Her kiss is as pure as wine.

<u>Together</u>

Let me lay within your arms.

Let me hear you say my name.

Let me trace your smile with my fingertip.

Nothing in the world matters more than you.

You are the only art I want to see.

You're the only poem I want to write.

You're all I want tonight.

Tomorrow

Forever

Most Beautiful

Most beautiful woman on the earth

Most beautiful woman ever born.

Voice of a siren

Hair like fire

What do I gotta do to prove my love for you?

What do I gotta do to get you to feel how I do?

Not just your body, but your mind makes me melt.

Not just your lips, but your eyes bring me to my knees.

Just seeing you is like believing in Eve in the garden of
Eden.

When She's Gone

Ain't no sunshine when she's gone.

There's no moonlight in my dreams.

I can't see the chocolate diamonds in her eyes.

I can't taste the red roses on her lips,

And I can't feel the white lily of her flesh

I just can't feel happy when she's not on my mind.

I can't be happy when she's not mine

Fallen Angel

She's got the smile of an angel.

Lips like a devil

Tongue of a queen

And a heart of a goddess

She's got that rock you want to roll with

She's got that flow you want to go with

She's got that love you want to take it slow with

She's one in a trillion and you know this.

Turn Me On

I want you to turn me on

I want you to blow my mind.

Be my sexual desire.

I want you to set my heart on fire.

Give me a fantasy

Give yourself to me.

Your skin is a drug.

Your body is a dream.

You got me hooked like a fiend.

<u>Light at The End</u>

In the darkest night

and lowest time

She shines above me like a guiding star.

My lovely north star

My one and only

She's one in a trillion.

There's no high higher than her.

Not a single woman greater than her

She's my inspiration and motivation.

I'd give her my undying dedication.

When I'm depressed, she's my medication.

She can put my love to the test.

She's always on my mind.

She's got me all obsessed.

My love I won't suppress.

I'm hers till my death.

Force of Nature

I lust for love.

A love I can't have.

A woman I can't own.

A goddess I can't control.

She's like a wildfire.

My beautiful flower child

Not Me

I might not be the one.

I might not be who you want.

But you're everything I need.

You're the beauty in my dreams.

With you I am free

You're all my heart can see.

I will want you till the end.

I will need you till I'm dead.

You're the poem stuck in my head.

I pray for you every night.

I will love you with all my might.

You're the moon high above me in the night.

<u>Falling for Her</u>

I dream of moon light.

But of a moon too far from me

I cannot be with her.

For she belongs far, far away from me.

High in the night sky

She shines her light upon my dreams.

Like Icarus of the sun

I fell for the moon.

Forever I shall fall.

For her I will give my all

What I Always Wanted

After every love song sung

After every kiss embraced

I dream a dream of your lovely face.

No matter how hard I try.

No matter how far I run.

My heartbeat races.

My feelings cannot hide.

A dream I've had since I was a boy.

A dream I'll have till the end of time.

Without Her

What's a heart without a beat?

A man without a hope?

A love without a dream?

That's how much she means to me.

She's the reason I go on.

She brings life to this poor vagabond.

She is the lily in a pond.

She is the foundation on which keeps me strong.

I feel nothing when she's gone.

__Alone__

I'm alone with you.

All I ever wanted was to be alone with you.

What I got was to be alone next to you.

You wouldn't look at me.

You couldn't see me.

But there I was alone with you.

All I wanted was to feel you next to me.

Not with my hands

Not with my arms

But with the one part of me I forgot I had

The one part of me that I have left to give.

The one part of me that was yours from the start.

Selene

What's a moon at night compared to her smile on my mind?

What are the clouds in the sky compared to the love deep within her eyes?

There's no drop of wine as fine as the taste of her sweet kiss.

It's the smile on my face when she's gone that I'll miss.

The sounds of rain falling is muted by the sounds of her laughter.

I was no one before I met her.

I'm left with nothing when she's gone.

Her reality is what all dreams should be.

I don't want ocean waves or beach sands.

But to lose myself in her hands.

Life

The beauty in irony of a short life for those who want to live.

And a road without end for those wishing to be dead

You could spend your life alone,

Or fill your life with love only to mourn for everything and everyone.

It's best to live life like a poker game,

And play your hand, win, or lose.

Fear not the outcome and be proud the decisions you choose.

My Muse

I turned my obsession into addiction into a constant affliction.

She's the queen of the night and a lovely dream under starlight.

Her eyes are the reasons why artist paint.

Her smile can make a mute stand up and sing.

Her heart is the reason a jeweler will turn gold into a ring.

These aren't just hollow words from another dime looking for a fling.

I only wish I had the strength to gaze upon her without breaking down onto my knees.

I can't look at her without passing harsh judgement on myself.

She's made of passion and beauty and all I see in me is a man made of flaws and broken things.

I need to get off my ass and be a man and remember I'm a king.

If I can love her and write a million words worthy of her name

If I give myself to her and admire her like the work of art that she is

Then I can be a better me and accomplish anything.

Lone Wolf

There's a red moon in the sky.

And a lone wolf is on the prowl

Lone wolf doesn't hunt, he takes.

Lone wolf doesn't want water, he wants a stronger drink.

Red moon in the sky

And one thing on his mind

Lone wolf's insides were a paradise that's suffered a drought.

Lone wolf's heart is a husk, it's dried up from doubt.

Red moon in the sky

Lone wolf cut himself to bleed out dry.

There's a red moon in the sky,

So he prays to his night owl.

With a daisy in her smile, she flies into the night sky.

Lone wolf calls for her, but she's singing to the stars far, far away.

Red moon in the sky

And lone wolf prowls in the dark

With a hunger without end, and a thirst he cannot quench.

Lone wolf dreams of amber ale and dark chocolate stout

Like the red moon in the sky

Lone wolf's madness bleeds out into his eyes.

Brother Wolf and Sister Moon

He walked out of his house into the backyard. The cold grass cracked beneath his bare feet. The cold wind turned into steam as it brushed against his nude skin. Tears seeped out of his bloodshot eyes as they stared at the full moon.

His anger deep within, pounded his heart like a drum. Boom, boom, boom, boom, his heart pounded as his teeth sharpened and grew. Hair sprouted all over his body. He dropped down to his knees and sank his clawed fists into the cold ground. He had become it, and he was no more a man, but a wolf.

The wolf ran into the forest behind the house. It ran with all its might. Its fur was wet with tears. It ran until it reached a clearing, and in this clearing, it howled at the moon. As it howled, the clouds closed in front of the moon forming a shadow.

She rose from the shadow on the ground. Her hair as dark as night and her skin pale and glowing as the moon. Her red lips smiled, and she whistled a tune to the wolf.

It came closer as she lowered to her knees. She wiped the tears from its eyes as it laid down in front of her. It closed it eyes and pressed its head against her hands.

He opened his eyes. No longer a wolf, he looked up to the moon and smiled. She was gone. He placed his hands over his heart as he whistled the tune she had whistled not long ago. He walked back to the house, shivering in the cold, his rage silenced.

Liberated

I sit in darkness hoping to find light.

I listen to your words hoping to find delight.

I remain in darkness in the shadow of your night.

I am not sorry for what I've done.

I do not repent for the victories I've won.

No chain shall ever imprison me,

No prison shall ever punish me.

My Dark Hope

Losing my mind.

No concept of time.

Am I yours or are you mine?

You're the light that I need.

You're the angel I pray to.

Do I stay or do I flee?

Beauty I need.

Lips that I crave.

You're the one I'm hoping for.

The Abyss

Into the nothing I go.

A great dark mystery on my horizon.

The never-ending road I travel is nothing more than a cliff.

Let me hang by a noose over the abyss.

I Am Sals

I can fly high like Icarus.

Journey far like Odysseus.

Spit a rhyme like Shakespeare.

Go balls deep like Ron Jeremy.

I'm as cheerful as Charon.

I can drink because my life goes on and on.

Like a never-ending song.

My high rings in like a gong.

My happiness goes up in smoke like Cheech and Chong.

Lime in My Drink

Two limes floating in my drink.

While I think.

Two limes soaking in my drink.

While my mind sinks.

Two limes drowning in my drink.

While my feelings get buried deep.

Happy Birthday Me

All I have is all I can't stand.

The fire, the gun powder, it's all pretty bland.

The same old band, the same one-night stand.

Another year older.

Another year stoner.

Pour another drink in the same sane glass.

Light the candles, start a mass.

Raise a toast to my dead ass.

Green

Green like envy.

Green of emerald.

Green serenity is all around me.

Green of the old.

Green is pure gold.

Green tranquility liberates me.

Roses

A black dead rose stands high.

Placed inside an empty beer bottle.

A red luscious rose hangs from the dead cold hands of the blushing bride as she slid into the furnace.

Dry brittle petals form a smile on a black rose.

Soft red velvet frowns against a cold dead corpse.

A black dead rose muses the artist as his brush dances on a blank canvas.

A luscious red rose is ignored as the mortician sets the gas before turning on the spark.

A black dead rose transforms into art.

A red luscious rose withers and burns and joins the bride in a pile of ash.

A Simple Equation

It's simple math.

Solve for ex.

Forget about those why's.

I'm not even sure why those other dudes even try.

I thought it was a mystery.

A final exam I couldn't pass.

I spent my whole life blind.

Not realizing I'm the one that's going to be there last.

And not just another dime stuck living in the past.

Pound

Put my fist through the mirror.

Put my fist through the wall.

So much anger burns inside me.

Till I'm feeling 2 foot small.

Point the finger at the enemy.

Not all ten, just the middle.

I'm to blame for my insanity.

Rhymes and riddles instead of feeling.

Let's play poker.

Devil's dealing.

All the rage keeps on bleeding.

As I bang against a glass ceiling.

Pray for Her

Lord I'm here, on my knees.

Hear my prayer, hear my plea.

Bring her back home to me.

I've been cold, I've been lone.

Without her love, I have no home.

Help me please.

Lord I'm here, on my knees.

Hear my prayer, hear my plea.

Bring her back home to me.

I am lost in the dark.

Without a light from my NorthStar.

I can't find my way back to her heart.

Lord I'm here, on my knees.

Hear my prayer, here my plea.

Bring her back home to me.

Break Free

Embrace the rage and face the pain.

But I will never wear my mask.

Like the moon in the night.

My words like stars will shine bright.

I will never hide my love again.

No bottle will contain me.

My silence will never retrain me.

I will never hide my love for you again.

Whether as a friend,

Or a lover in your bed.

I will never hide my love for you again.

When the night is cold,

And love runs cold.

I'll be here for you in the end.

<u>Not Your Time</u>

If he had a face, he could express his pain. If he had tears ducts, he could cry. The scythe shook within his tightly gripped bone hand. The reaper knelt beside her cold lifeless body and restarted her broken heart. As he walked away, he whispered with all his sorrow, "Forgive me. no matter how many times you call me, no matter how times you hurt yourself. It's not your time, not by a long shot."

I.O.U.

I wanted to end it when I was just beginning.

Till I saw your rose like lips smiling.

It was blinding like the sun.

Like Icarus I wanted to reach you.

I built wings just to get to you.

The higher I rose, the harder I had to fall.

My only regret was that I wasn't worthy.

But still you stirred something inside of me.

Thanks to you I know life is worth the hurting.

When I'm at my darkest, I picture you smiling.

When I'm at my lowest, I remember you laughing.

I owe you for my smile.

I owe you for my laugh.

I owe you for my will.

I owe you for my desire.

I owe you for my hope.

I owe you for my dreams.

Earworm

I'll never,

move on.

I can never,

Let go and go on.

Because you are a dream.

Keeping me in my bed.

It's a feeling,

I'll hold on to till I'm dead.

Because you're everything to me.

Like a song I can't get out of my head,

I'll smile,

and I'll dance.

All because of what you do to me.

Unnatural

Gravity pulls you in.

The wind pushes you forward.

The earth stops spinning.

and all the chaos settles into peace.

The empty feeling goes away.

It warms the coldest night.

<u>Childish Love</u>

I'm staring at lines on a paper thinking which words are
good enough to describe you.

I'm staring at the point of a pencil trying to trace every line
and curve of your face.

You're my muse, my high, my rush, my art.

If you were the sun, each planet would be a piece of my
broken heart.

I want to live our future, but I also want to hit the restart.

To be a kid on the playground to hand you a dandelion.

To push you on the swings instead of pushing you away.

It's a perfect life to live because you're perfect in every
flawed way.

Without You

I can't go on.

I don't want to move on.

I don't see the point.

I can't find the reason.

I know what's missing.

I know why I can never feel complete.

There's no world without you girl.

No warmth, no life.

I'm just dead inside without you.

You were my spark.

The light at the end of the tunnel.

It don't make sense.

Take away you and all my senses go with you.

I can't live like this.

Longing

He sat at the bar like a stone gargoyle. The music over the loudspeaker started with the tapping of the symbols. The symbols of the drums rattled in sync with his shaky nerves. The beat of the drums raced with his heart as his anxiety rose. The singer's warm baritone voice echoed as he sang each word with more fire and passion than a man should feel for a woman. His red eyes boiled as he stared at his steaming hot black coffee. The muscles in his face tightened as he fought to bury his emotions. He wanted to destroy the whole world, knowing that she was no longer in it.

My Hope

You are the flame on a prayer candle.

The light at the end of the tunnel.

At the end of every bad relationship, I think of you.

It gives me hope and renews my faith.

After every bad apple, I know you're still the one.

The one I don't regret, the girl I'll never forget.

Mr. Wrong

This isn't jealousy.

Nor am I coveting.

I'm simply acknowledging the one thing I never could see.

That I'm a good man, a better man than most.

I don't hate him or blame him.

I just know better that you're worth more.

You deserve more than some time, part time, or full time.

You deserve overtime and more.

You want love, you want loyalty.

All you have to do is choose me.

If you want me, you got me.

I was always yours,

And I'll always will be.

Victorious

Rosey lips and brown eyes like a Hershey's kiss haunting me.

An addiction and obsession.

A smile I can't get out of my mind.

A beauty to last till the end of time.

Creamy soft skin, just thinking about you is a sin.

Being with you is a win.

Victory and defeat, every time I see you.

You knock me dead off my feet.

A sweat dream covered in bruises and scars.

The perfect woman by far.

No Me Dejas

No me dejes mi amor.

No te vayas sin yo ver a tu sonrisa.

Si tengo que esperar a que regreses te esperare por siempre.

Me quedare aqui durmiendo y sonando contigo.

Mientras tanto llegaran otras muchachas.

Seran mi trago y mi droga.

Para no dejarme sentir.

Por que sin ti, solo voy a sufrir.

My Own Worst Enemy

Thirty-five to life of solitary confinement.

Followed by an eternity in purgatory.

What did I do to deserve this punishment?

What was my crime, what was my sin?

Why did I do this to myself?

Why did I condemn myself?

Why do I hate myself so much?

Why am I so hard on myself?

Why can't I see the key to my freedom?

Why can't I open this cage that I put myself in?

Why do I keep comparing myself to him?

Him, who cheated on you.

Him, who beat on you.

Him, who wasn't even in love with you.

Him, who wasn't obsessed with you.

Was it wrong to make you smile?

Was it wrong to make you laugh?

Was it wrong to be in love with you?

Why do I expect to get everything when I have absolutely
nothing to give?

That Empty Feeling

Life without you is like being a fish in a fishbowl.

I can feel the waves of the water carrying me, but I'm still cut off from the sea.

Like an amputee feeling a phantom limb,

I'm living with a phantom heart.

It beats, it rumbles, but it's not there and I'm feeling nothing.

Moths In The Night

She was a raging fire who was as peaceful as a prayer candle.

We were moths dancing around her.

One of us will get to feel her warmth.

Most of us will burn within her embrace.

Every night without her is cold and black.

In Dreams

In my dreams I can feel.

It's there you're alone with me.

I feel safe and free as your love wraps around me.

In my dreams, in my dreams, in my dreams I can see you were meant for me.

In my sleep, in my dreams, in my heart you're here with me.

Love and Lust

Give me a dream.

Make me a fantasy.

Let me admire my reflection in the center of your chocolate eyes.

Bring me to my knees so I can worship you at the thighs.

You came into my life like a surprise.

You're like the sun, you make my heart rise.

A devil and an angel.

A mistress and a wife.

Cut my heart out with a knife.

Own my soul for the rest of my life.

Your Face

Help me find the beat,

So I can rhyme and flow.

You're like an angel.

I thought I should let you know.

My muse and desire.

I cannot let you go.

There's no one else like you.

A one in a billion fo sho.

You bring a smile to my face.

You're the only one I want to embrace.

Like music and wine,

Loving you is in good taste.

I want to see you in leather and lace.

Every time I dream,

I always see your face.

Rush

I want to feel my blood rush throughout my body.

I want to feel my flesh burn like a moth in the flame.

I want to feel the natural high I find within your smile.

I want to feel more alive than I have felt after the first time
I saw you.

The only thing more beautiful than seeing the sun in the
blue sky,

Is seeing the chocolate sparkle in your eyes.

The only thing more beautiful than a song lyric is the pink
of your lips.

102 Degrees Fahrenheit

It starts with a fever.

A fire burning through each vein.

An obsession.

A need.

A desire.

The moth and flame.

Icarus and the Sun.

Nothing else will satisfy this craving.

No one could take your place.

Every sleepless night I'm haunted by your face.

No appetite or thirst.

Just my obsession with each passing day gets worse and worse.

From Transylvania With Love

He walked into the strip club and sat at a single table with one chair. He took off his black overcoat and hung it on the back of his chair. He appeared to be a man of twenty-seven, but had the presence of an old soul. He had a pencil-thin mustache and slicked-back, dark brown hair.

She was twenty-six and went by the name 'Flower'. Brown eyes, auburn hair, voluptuous and curvaceous body. She was the only woman in the club he would ever look at. She wasn't a dancer, just a drink server in a provocative outfit.

He would order a Cabernet Sauvignon, and she would serve it. He would recite poems to her, and she would smile and blush at them. He would tell a joke and she would laugh. Genuinely laugh. A laughter as beautiful as her soul.

All the dancers knew not to waste their time approaching him. Every time Flower walked away, he would take a locket out of his pocket. In the locket was a withered flower on one side and a black-and-white photo that strongly resembled the lovely drink server.

He would watch her work and dream of making love to her. Holding her in his arms, running his big strong hands around her waist. He wanted to hear the sweet music of her heavy breathing. He wanted to smell her hair like petals on a rose. His chest rose and fell. His veins dilated and his blood shot through every artery, like rushing water throughout his entire body. His mouth salivated. His teeth sharpened. He was hungry for her.

He could picture her lying naked in bed. In a flowery dress, lying in a field of flowers. He could picture her throat pulsating with life. He felt empty. Hollowed out. A living, breathing husk. Almost starving to death without actually dying.

He pictured a cold and gray world without her in it. He pictured a field of dead, withered flowers. His heart sank to the bottom of his stomach. He gasped for air as if he had stopped breathing. He wiped a blood-stained tear from his eye.

He watched her solemnly all night. He hummed an ancient song forgotten by time. He had signaled her with a shaky hand for the check. As he got up, he handed her what he owed, plus the tip.

He took one last gulp from his wine before telling her, "I lost you once, and it broke me. It turned my heart to dust. I have watched the moon come and go for what seems like an eternity. I have seen empires rise and fall. A life without you is like a lifetime in purgatory. I bid you farewell, my flower child."

She was taken back, unsure what to say. Something stirred within her, a longing to be with him. A desire to return the sentiment. She felt a familiarity and comfort at his sight.

Outside, the parking lot was empty with the exception of one black car. He sat on the hood and waited for the sun to rise. As dark turned into light, his pale skin became warm and olive in color. Steam rose from every orifice and pore on his body.

She walked out of the club. No longer Flower, Mina saw her secret admirer sitting on the hood of his car. He turned around and saw her for the final time. His skin cracked and slowly disintegrated into ash.

All Mina could see was the man fade into the wind with the rising sun.

Please Don't Go

Please don't go.

Please don't go.

Don't go walk out that door.

Don't you leave my heart on the floor.

Don't you know that I'm all yours?

Please don't go.

Baby, please don't go.

I want to be yours all night.

I want to hold you with all my might.

You're my reason for sight.

In the dark, you're my light.

You're the only thing I want to bite.

With you baby, I'm alright.

What Keeps Me Going

I have nothing to lose,

And everything to gain.

Your name is the only thing keeping me sane.

I want to build a future,

And travel back to the past.

To go back years ago when I first hear you laugh.

I'm yours since the start.

I'm yours till the end.

I want to be your lover and best friend.

I don't want to own you.

I don't want to control you.

You'd never be mine.

I just want to be yours.

Angel

Angel, your love is like a light.

Angel, it burns in the dark so bright.

Angel, you're a sunflower in my sight.

All I want to do is make you smile.

All I want to do is be yours for a while.

If you want me,

If you need me,

I'm all yours.

The Passenger

I look to the open road.

I drive and drive and drive.

I look to my right,

And you're not there.

Your scent lingers.

My hand reaches out.

In hopes to touch your fingers.

But you're not there.

You're not in your seat.

You're not in your spot.

You're not in your place in my heart.

I can see ahead,

But I cannot see your face.

I'm racing to get home,

But you're not there.

So I keep on driving to my doom.

I drive, I drive.

I strive and I dream.

I dream of a goddess, a queen. An angel.

While I drive and go on.

With or without you I go on.

Her

A rose on the moon,

Is only as beautiful as a sunflower in full bloom.

At the sight of her I swoon.

At the sight of her I drop to my knees.

When I'm with her I am free.

With her I can be.

She's the only one I want to see.

She gets all my worship and praise.

For her I'll stay.

For her I yearn.

For her I will burn.

At First

I wish to see you in the sun.

Your smile in the moon.

I wish to hear your laughter on the wind.

I wish to feel your skin like grass in an open field.

I wish to see you as a hawk, free, high, and above me.

I wish to see you in my dreams and in my arms.

I wish to see myself in your heart.

I've wished all these things from the start.

From the very first time I saw you.

I knew.

I knew all I should ever need

<u>Wish</u>

I wish you could see me,

And see what I dream.

I dream of you and me,

And all the things we could be.

If only I could exist.

Because you're the peace that I miss.

You're the flower I want to kiss.

You're the angel I can't resist.

<u>My Intoxication</u>

I'm drunk off you.

I'm high on you.

Sunflower fumes.

You're my hope, you're my doom.

I'll drive miles just to see you.

I'll do anything to get you in my room.

You're an angel and a devil.

The flower child and the rebel.

Every time I see you, I hear church bells.

Being without you is a hell.

I love you with every cell.

The Plains and The Flowers

Ohpichiwa was a humble but lonely spirit of the plains. He wandered the land in a time before the existence of man. He often lay in the grass admiring the sun. He felt that the sun, high above in the sky, was the only thing as lonely as he was.

Ohpichiwa would sing to the sun. He would dance for the sun. He would often cry when the clouds came and blocked out the sun.

On a fateful day, Ohpichiwa heard soft singing from a distance. He followed the sound as if the wind were blowing him toward the source.

Ohpichiwa was familiar with the grass and trees, but as the song drew closer, he noticed strange, yet beautiful and colorful growth, springing from the ground. These were the first flowers of the land. As he got closer to the source of the singing, Ohpichiwa was stunned and amazed. He felt the world spinning as he looked upon Fluwatu, a plant spirit.

Fluwatu was singing to the sun, and dancing as well. Wherever her feet landed, more and more flowers of blues, whites, reds, and purples bloomed. Fluwatu stopped when she saw Ohpichiwa. She had always thought of herself as alone and loved only the sun.

The two were immediately drawn to each other—as if the winds commanded them toward one another. They were inseparable from that day forth. They would sing and dance together. Their love made the land flourish with luscious green grass and a rainbow array of flowers.

One day, the clouds came and blocked out the sun. The winds blew harder than ever, and instead of rain, the water froze and fell as the first snowfall of the land. The harsh weather was killing all of Fluwatu's flowers. Eventually, the first snows killed Fluwatu.

Ohpichiwa was sad and heartbroken. He had to bury his love in the same field where they first met. As it continued to snow, Ohpichiwa kneeled down and sang songs to his love's grave. Eventually, Ohpichiwa froze and was encased in snow to sleep for a very long time.

Eventually, the clouds went away, and the sun returned, melting all the snow and freeing Ohpichiwa from his icy shackles. He stared at the sun, angry and confused. Why had the sun saved him? Why did the sun not let him stay asleep to dream of his Fluwatu?

When he looked down, he noticed a single yellow flower blooming from Fluwatu's grave. It was her last gift to him. The flower was yellow like the sun, and it was only fitting that he named the flower after the one thing they had both loved. It was the first sunflower.

Red

Rose red beauty in my head.

Red siren angel in my bed.

She's a thought.

She's a dream.

She's a mother and a queen.

Rose lips and my kisses on her hips.

Red flowing dress brings me to my knees to confess.

She's amazing.

She's fantastic.

A euphoric dream most orgasmic.

Lost and Found

A man wandered alone at night. He reached the beach and found a boat. He hopped into the boat and paddled out to sea. Before he knew it, he was lost in the darkness of night. He wasn't sure what to do or where to go.

But then, he heard the voice of an angel singing. He looked up and saw a shining star—the biggest star in the nighttime sky. He paddled toward the shining star and found himself on a small, lonely island. On this island stood a red-haired siren singing, leading the man to shore.

The man walked up to the siren, and she embraced him in her arms. The man was entranced by the smell of her fiery red hair and smoothness of her warm skin. There, the man no longer felt lost. There, the man felt he belonged. There, the man lived happily ever after.

My Inner Peace

Neither the land, sea, nor air could compare to you.

If I wanted beauty, I'd chose you over a museum,

If I wanted peace, I'd listen to your laughter instead of music.

You're my drug of choice.

The drink that turns me into a freak.

You're my zen.

My higher plane of existence.

You're the light at the end of my tunnel.

My happy ending and my dream.

You're too good to be true.

I'm all yours till the end.

You're my obituary when I'm dead.

Be Mine

I want to fade into you.

I want to sleep in the shade under you.

I want to rock to the soothing sounds made by you.

Build my dreams out of your smile.

Come into my life and drive me wild.

Come close to me and set me on fire.

Be my muse, my desire.

My One Wish

I wish you could see me.

See the man that I could be.

See me the way I see you.

I wish you loved me too.

I'd do anything for you.

I want to be everything to you.

I know I should move on.

But I rather much hold on.

No matter how much it hurts me.

No matter how many times it breaks me.

My feelings never change.

I will love you every day.

New Sensation

I feel like a blind man seeing the sun for the first time every time I see your face.

It's like hearing the wind blow every time I listen to you speak.

Your soft touch takes me over like waves flowing over the sandy beach.

My blood runs wild like horses in the plain.

My knees crumble down like sand falling through the hourglass.

I feel more alive than a newborn baby when you're around.

My Goddess

I wish to greet you like the sun greets the earth.

I wish to raise you higher than the pedestal you sit on.

I wish to show you off like the work of art you are.

I wish to bask in your intoxicating aura.

You are Dionysus.

You are Huitaca.

You are a force of nature.

You are nature itself.

The grass praises at your soft feet.

The wind caresses your glowing skin.

You are the snake queen, deadly and beautiful.

Your heart rumbles like the stampede of stallions.

Your voice soothes like waves on the beach.

Chaos

To see you smile drives me wild.

Like a drug running through my blood.

I'm high on your laughter.

Making my heart race faster and faster.

My beautiful disaster

Apart of Me

There's a song in my head.

There's a smile in my eyes.

Her voice echoes in my mind.

She's the missing piece of my life.

She cannot see me.

She has no faith in me.

But I still believe in her.

She's everything to me.

I'm a nobody to her.

But I cannot stop loving her.

She's all I want.

She's all I need.

She's the missing piece of me.

I may have false hope.

But it's better than no hope.

She's in my every thought.

She's in all my dreams.

She's what missing.

She's the greatest part of me.

<u>My Beginning and End</u>

You are my first and last thought.

You are my only desire.

You're the only future worth seeing.

You make me want to be a better human being.

Without you I'm numb.

With you I'm free and full of feeling.

There's no experience I want to enjoy without you.

There's no future I want to live without you.

No, I'm not down and feeling blue.

I'm just in limbo and not feeling anything at all.

I bang my fist against the wall.

I sit here trapped waiting for you to call.

To You

To the most beautiful woman on earth.

You are beautiful.

You are sexy.

You drive me wild.

You make me insatiable.

I'm always dreaming of your face.

I'm always picturing you in lace.

I don't want you to be good.

I just want you bad.

Seeing you is like an adrenaline rush.

I feel helpless and weak without your touch.

Demeter

You are the flower.

You are the sun.

You are the celebration that I pray for every day.

I'm dreaming of your face.

I'm picturing you draped in lace.

You are my poison.

You are my drug.

You are my addiction that brings me up to break me down.

You are my weakness.

You are my strength.

You give me feelings.

Give me your sweet embrace.

I'll do anything for you.

Anything you want.

Just be in my life.

Be my every dream.

You are everything I need.

Scarlett

I point my car towards the sun.

I'm driven to have some fun.

I'm lonely without you hun.

Music blaring.

I keep staring.

Watching the asphalt pass beneath me.

I wish you wanted to see me.

I'm driving as far as I can because you're never near me.

On Fire

Hey little miss fire.

You are what I desire.

Throw me on the pyre.

Don't call me no liar.

I am just a moth.

Feeling a whole lot hot.

You had caught my heart.

All from the start.

Love you till I'm dead.

Love you till the end.

Cara Mia

Little miss midnight.

Girl child of the moon.

As beautiful as a black rose.

As peaceful as a coffin.

A black dahlia in the night.

I will love you with all my might.

A mother and a queen.

A daughter and my sin.

To adore you I drop to my knees.

Be a viper, I want you to bite me.

Be my freedom, my sweet release.

Lust

I want to hear your voice.

I want to feel your skin.

To feel your teeth on my skin.

My beautiful original sin.

A goddess of night and fire.

My sexy secret desire.

I am a moth in the night.

I want to feel your flames,

And let the heat embrace me.

Set me to the flame.

So I can worship your name.

Day Dreaming

I have my head in the clouds.

I want to say your name out loud.

I'm soring high.

Just from having you on my mind.

Wishing you were by my side.

I feel weightless.

I fell hopeless.

I want to trip and enjoy this ride.

Like watching the tides on the beach.

Your hand is far from my reach.

You're the only happiness that I seek.

You are my nirvana.

My highest peak.

My Ale

Watching the amber flow out like a waterfall.

Sooth me over like the relief after the storm.

Every feeling I bottled up pours out.

Every memory that haunts me is erased.

Washed over like sand on the beach.

I am the glass.

Hoping to fall and shatter against the bar floor.

I am the rock at the bottom that waves crash against.

You are what you eat.

I am what I drink.

A medicinal poison.

My substitute for who I'm missing.

The only joy to touch my lips.

I drink it up, sip by sip.

The Night

The night is cold and black,

and reminds me of you.

The moon is bright and beautiful,

and reminds me of you.

I don't cry at night because I'm lonely.

I cry at night because everything reminds me of you.

Thoughts of You

The black of the sky.

The lovely glow of the moon and stars.

The cold air.

Creatures of the night: black cats, owls, and coyotes.

The peacefulness of a world locked in silence.

Your hair.

Your eyes.

Mistress of the night.

Awake or asleep; I dream of you.

Nighttime is my happy hour.

Because all of it reminds me of you.

Set Me Free

I don't want to sleep.

I don't want to rest.

I want to run with the wolves,

and howl at the moon.

Sing to the moon.

Worship and admire the moon.

I don't want to sleep.

I don't want to dream.

I want to live in the night.

Dance, play, and enjoy every hour of the night.

Embrace the darkness.

Welcome its cold mystery.

One

I'm a quadriplegic scratching at my phantom limbs.

I'm a body without a soul.

I got soul but I ain't got nobody.

I can't tell if I'm dead or just numb.

The fact that I let you go shows that I'm quite dumb.

I cannot see the light.

I cannot feel its hope.

Closest thing to being with you is smoking a whole lotta dope.

I'm at my end.

It's at the bottom of a rope.

I can live without you but baby I can't cope.

My Drug of Choice

Please smile for me.

All I need is to see your smile,

And I'll be fine for a while.

Let me see you smile.

I want to fall; I want to feel myself melt.

Let me hear your voice.

Say anything.

I want to feel my stress fall of my shoulders.

I want to feel high like a bird in the sky.

Let me look into your eyes.

Let me see myself in the middle of your pupil.

My reflection in a chocolate diamond.

That's all I want.

That's all I need.

It's my addiction.

My self-medication.

My drug of choice is to be with you.

Jonesin'

Tick tock

Tick tock

With each tick my world withers and cracks.

Peace by peace until I snap.

Tick tock

Tick tock

I try to run; I try to hide.

The thought of you I buried deep inside.

But with each ticking of the clock.

You're resurrected in my head.

Under each thought.

Behind every dream.

I think of a flower and it makes me want to scream.

Tick tock

Tick tock

Underneath it all

At the very core

With every bit of my soul

I am yours but you're not mine.

You are the foundation of my mind.

Tick tock

Tick tock

Every obsessive second.

Every dismal minute.

I think of you.

I pine for you.

I drown myself in wine,

Because I'm without you.

Tick tock

Tick tock

Chemically Unbalanced

Alone

By myself

In solitaire

I am what I eat.

I what I drink.

Eat me and grow

Drink me and shrink

My brain is rewired.

It's made of what I'm taking.

Serotonin

Dopamine

Ethanol

Tetrahydrocannabinol

I'm up.

I'm down.

Sometimes I'm a clown.

I get around.

Gotta stop to make sure,

My psyche is sound.

I feel like a river.

I feel light as air.

My All

I want to grow you a field of flowers.

I want to build you a house to make a home.

I want to draw your smile in the clouds.

I hope that one day you will accept it from me.

I want to give you gold and silver.

Golden memories to last a lifetime.

Silver hairs from my head as we grow old.

Please accept what I have to offer you.

My heart and soul.

And if I could, I'd give you the moon.

I'd write music and poems to make you swoon.

I'd live my life for you and no one else.

All I want in return is you and nothing less.

Obsession Confession

I don't want to think of you.

But I can't help it.

I don't want to dream of you.

But I can't help it.

Million fish in the sea but none like you.

I should move on.

But I can't.

I won't.

I wouldn't know how to if I wanted to.

I fell for you like Icarus for the sun.

I fell from you like Lucifer from heaven.

If I'm lucky you'll be the death of me.

If I want to be happy, I need you next to me.

Dark Desire

Every day is dark.

Every day sucks.

I want something beautiful in my life.

All I want is you.

My life has no meaning.

My life has no purpose.

But the idea of being with you is a dream worth chasing.

My hope of one day being with you keeps me going.

If I could get you to notice me.

If I could get you to want me.

All I want is a life for you and me.

Insomnia

Here I lay staring at my ceiling.

Here I stay thinking of you my darling.

What can I do when I cannot sleep?

What can I do when I can't dream of you?

You're in my every thought.

Even when I don't want you to.

You're my every desire.

My fantasy.

My happily ever after.

All I can do is remember the good times we had.

All I can do is fantasize of the life we'll never have.

Even when you're not in my life,

You're still keeping me up at night.

I wish you could accept me.

So I could love you with all my might.

Ageless

You are the ocean and the trees.

Beautiful and timeless.

You are a work of art.

Frozen and preserved for all time.

You are the music and the rhyme.

Never old and always welcomed.

You are a drug.

You're my brand of rum.

Sunshine of Your Love

I thought I was staring at the sun.

I thought I was seeing flowers.

But I was blinded by the sight.

I was high on my own delight.

I was hooked on your smile.

I felt my soul set on fire.

If I were a bee, you would definitely be my queen.

I felt humbled and I dropped to my knees.

The chaos in my mind was at ease.

If you were Helen, I would launch a thousand ships to sail the seas.

I'd do anything to see you smile.

I'd crawl on my hands and feet for miles and miles.

If it would make you happy.

If it would make you notice me.

If I were a moth, I'd gladly set myself on fire from the heat of my desire.

I'd die with a smile just for being near you for a while.

<u>But You</u>

I have the sun in my face.

I have the wind in my hair.

I can hear the music in my ears.

I have the words in my throat.

I have everything I want, but you.

I have my health.

I can see a long road of life ahead of me.

I earn my living.

I spend what I make.

I can have anything I want but you.

There's a smile on my face.

There's love in my heart.

I can feel anything I want but you.

Living on The Edge

I want to go to the edge of the world.

I want to throw myself off.

I want your name to be my last word.

I lived my life an open book.

Every chapter inspired by you.

Every chapter dedicated to you.

Every word written for you.

No Matter

No matter who you are with.

No matter who you love.

I will always love you.

God, fate, the universe tells me to move on.

I can't, I won't, I wait patiently for my turn.

Not my turn to be with you.

But for a chance to prove that I deserve you more

<u>Farewell</u>

You're out of my life,

But not out of my heart.

My brain is on fire.

Thinking of all the sweet words I want to say to you.

If I did something to displease you,

Please forgive me.

If I loved you too much,

For that I won't apologize for.

I move forward with my life.

But you're always on my mind.

Mariachi's Muse

In a little cantina, in a little pueblo with dirt-covered roads, played a mariachi. Julano played guitar with his two childhood friends who weren't as talented as him. The mariachi never thought much of himself or his music. Every night, they played popular songs that the cantina patrons requested. Every night, the requests were the same. Every night, they played the same set of songs for the same cantina patrons.

The cantina smelled of a mix of redwood furniture, adobe walls, piss-warm beer, and tequila. It was badly lit, but the stage lights blinded Julano. Not being able to see the expressions on his faceless crowd just added to the monotony of playing every night. The same songs, followed by the same reactionary applause from the faceless patrons, took a toll on Julano.

As the weekends went by and repeated themselves, an emptiness grew inside him. His fingers shook in protest at playing the same meaningless chords. His face could no longer form a smile. The mariachi grabbed a bottle of tequila every weekend night before he could pick up his guitar. Eventually, the lack of passion within him became the lack of passion heard and felt in the music they played repeatedly. Soon, patrons lost their desire to listen to live music played at the cantina [bar]. The emptiness inside Julano manifested itself into an empty cantina for the mariachi to play in.

On a mundane and silent night, Ella sat by the bar, drinking red wine by herself. The cantina was empty, the stage lights were off, and nothing could keep Julano's brown eyes off her tan face. Julano played a faster tempo as his heart pounded against the bones of his chest cavity. She did nothing but bob her head. Ella had a soft smile as she watched the mariachi play. Julano felt more alive than he ever had in his life. He swayed his hips as she rocked her shoulders from side to side. His two companions were taken by surprise, but immediately followed with their playing. The bartender cleaned a glass as his attention was brought toward the music playing. The bored waitress danced lightly as the few patrons tapped their feet gently. As the trio played on, at least two night wanderers came in and had a drink.

At the end of the set, three more patrons came in, and one very drunk patron left the cantina with a señorita that clearly wasn't his wife. Julano looked at the border of the stage and saw a few pesos and a shot of tequila from the patrons. His two friends wiped sweat from their faces as they hadn't played like that in a long time. Julano turned his back to put down his guitar, but when he stood back up, all he saw was Ella's finished wine glass.

Julano nervously rushed to the bar to ask the bartender the name of the girl. To which the bartender responded impolitely, "Qual mora? [What girl]"

Julano normally walked home with his bandmates, but tonight, he decided to walk alone on a longer route so he could think about his mysterious fan. There were very few street lamps. His pueblo felt asleep. He walked alone in the dark, dreaming of this mysterious chula [cute girl]. He had flashes of black wavy hair and soft, light brown skin. He couldn't tell how much of his vision devina [divine] was memory, and how much was just his imagination filling in the blanks that he couldn't remember.

He held his arms up like he was about to start dancing. Only his fingers moved. He was imagining that he was playing his guitar. The more he thought of her, the clearer the melody in his head was. He imagined her singing, but he had no idea what her voice sounded like. He couldn't imagine the sound of her voice, but he could sense it. He felt the lyrics she was mouthing.

His eyes were closed, and he had a childlike smile on his face. The song was clear in his head. Her song was fresh on his mind. All he had to do was get home to write it down.

On his way, he found his two tios, Edgar and Nestor, passed out from their card game. He quietly snuck up and took their unfinished bottle of tequila. An old love song was playing on their radio.

Julano sang to the song's rhythm, "Give me a few loving words and I'll give you a song.

A love song that's yours and yours alone."

Julano kept walking, letting the words dance inside his head. He saw one of the bar patrons coming home to his angry wife. He tried to kiss her, but her chankla [slipper] slapped the other woman's lipstick off his face.

"Give me your hands and I'll get your glass slippers dancing.

Don't ask me about my past.

Don't worry about the nights before and the other women I can't remember.

For I was meant for you and you alone."

The song kept coming together piece by piece. Julano soon found his little primo Maicolino sneaking out late. He quietly followed him and saw him throwing pebbles at young Navana's window.

154

"Keep your heart open like the window at night.

Let my feelings for you sneak in like the nighttime breeze.

The moon will shine on my dreams.

My sweet dreams of you, and you alone."

Julano smiled at the sight of young love. He was happy for his little primo for coming out to visit the prettiest girl in town.

"PINCHE CHINGERO! Te voy a rompe la cabeza y chingar tu puta madre!" [EXPLICITING EXPLICIT! I'm going to break open your head and explicit your explicit mother!]

Navana's father was not too pleased at the sight of her young gentleman caller. Maicolino ran as fast as he could. The old man chased after him, so Julano intervened. He pretended to be drunk and tripped the old man.

"Maldito boracho! Te voy a meter ese pinche quitara en el culo!"

"Puta madre!" said Julano, as he began to run as fast as he could. Thankfully, Maicolino returned the favor and got the old man's attention. The old man chased Maicolino as long as he could, until the young Lothario hopped over a wall. The chase was over, and the old man had no choice but to return home. When he turned around, Julano was nowhere to be found.

The inspired song writer kept on his way, looking behind him for the old man. He finally got home and started writing… and drinking. The next day, Julano was hungover and unable to get out of bed, except when he had to run to the bathroom to throw up. The day after that, he was able to meet with his bandmates.

They were shocked and amazed. They were impressed with the song their band leader had written. They practiced day and night. Julano encouraged his band mates to have fun and contribute to the song.

It was finally Friday. The cantina had a significant number of patrons. Two married couples were enjoying drinks and looking forward to listening to the mariachis after hearing about their last performance. One drunk patron was with a señorita who wasn't his wife, but the red chankla mark across his face was definitely his wife's.

The band smiled and joked as they got ready for their set. Several patrons teased the band to get started faster.

The pleas and jokes only excited the band. They weren't used to being so well received. They couldn't wait to start their set. The band was ready, and they gave a quick glance at one another. They were feeling good and confident.

They started playing a popular love song, but they played it livelier, more up-tempo. The small crowd got out of their chairs. They started cheering and whistling at the band. The band then went straight into a typical dance song. At that point, the patrons began to stomp and clap.

The excitement was electric. Everyone and the mariachis were having the time of their lives. Julano's senses were amplified by the overwhelming emotions in the cantina and just like that, time seemed to have stopped. The music was replaced by a deafening silence that only Julano could hear. Everyone in the cantina—the patrons, the bartender, the waitresses, the mariachis— everyone was frozen solid. There was a dead feeling, an emptiness within Julano's stomach. He felt nervous, scared, and nauseous. The air was hot and stale.

Then, at that very same moment, Julano heard the soft sounds of harps playing. A sweet cool breeze blew away Julano's negative feelings. Julano watched Ella slowly walk into the cantina and go straight to the bar. Julano's thoughts went silent. All he could do was watch her walk to the bar, and smile politely at the bartender, who immediately poured her a glass of wine.

Julano began playing the introduction to the new song that he and his bandmates had written. He was like a possessed mariachi, unaware of his actions. His bandmates were confused as they were already halfway through their current song. But one by one, each bandmate started to switch into the new song. The cantina patrons were caught off guard as they had never heard the song before. Julano's eyes were locked onto Ella who was now just watching the small crowd.

Like a lover whispering into their partner's ear, Julano began to sing the first few lines. The few ladies there swooned at the declaration of pure love resonating within the lyrics. One couple cuddled, another slow danced, the one drunk patron rubbed the chankla mark on his face. He gave his señorita money for her drinks and went home to his wife. The smell of piss-warm beer and tequila in the air was replaced with amor … love. The passion in the cantina was so hot that the very temperature of the room went up, among other things.

The song ended and the applause began. Julano and his bandmates felt like rockstars, if rock and roll music had existed in their time. The bartender rewarded the mariachis with shots of tequila, while the waitresses handed out shots for the patrons as well. Soon, everyone in the cantina were raising their shots to honor the mariachis' playing and the amazing love-inspiring song they had just performed.

As everyone threw back their shots, Julano became a passenger in his own body. All he could do was watch the distance between him and Ella get shortened. The bartender noticed what was going to happen and was trying to finish celebrating with the patrons before intervening.

He locked onto her eyes as he said, "Hola, me llamo Julano Geraldo Evelio Hilario Alfonso De Florentino and that song, I wrote for you and only you."

Ella had a bewildered look on her face.

Confused, Julano asked, "Did you not like my song, your song?"

She pointed at her ears, and shook her head no. She had a sad and helpless look on her face, as the bartender placed his hand on her shoulder and gestured with his head for her to leave.

The bartender paused, took a deep breath before saying, "I'm sorry to be the bearer of disappointing news chamaco, pero [kid, but] Ella is my niece. She was born deaf. Very few people in this pueblo know who she is or about her inability to hear. My brother, her papa, and her, prefer discretion. A lot of people won't understand her situation and could possibly treat her as if she were crippled, unintelligent, or even a freak."

"I don't understand."

"I know you don't. She's quite brilliant. Loves to read. Did impressively well according to her private teacher. One of the sisters from the church is deaf and teaches other deaf children. She doesn't have a social life outside the family, but she does love to watch people. She's a very insightful observer. She also knows to blend in and read lips. I let her hang out here so she can feel like a 'normal' person. She can't hear the music, but she can mimic the other patrons and tends to bob her head and sometimes even dance."

"Okay, but can I talk to her? Get to know her?"

The bartender shook his head no. "What I told you is all you'll get to know of her. I'm sorry, but if you try to talk to her, she won't be able to hear you and I can only surmise that you don't know sign language, which is a form of communication using hand gestures. I highly suggest that you just give …"

Before he could finish giving his advice, Julano finished what was left in her wine glass, followed by random shots of tequila that were left on the bar. He thanked the bartender and solemnly walked back to his band mates. They were confused by the look of defeat on his face, until he wiped away the tears and faked a smile.

Shortly after that night, Julano went on to write more songs, thinking about Ella. Each weekend, the cantina drew more and more patrons. Eventually, Julano and his band mates saved up their money to travel to other pueblos to perform. Julano never saw Ella ever again, but neither did he forget how beautiful she had looked drinking her wine by the bar.

<u>El Fin</u>

Mi Dios Te Paga and Que Te Bendiga!

May God Reward you and Bless You!

I want to give one last thank you to everyone who bought and read my book.

Thank you for choosing to buy and hopefully read every word and emotion that I wrote down these past ten years working on my craft.

This isn't the end, it's just the beginning, and I hope to put out many more books, stories, and poems before my time comes.

All I ask is that you like, review, and post all over social media for me. Please hit up all the online sites where my book and e-book are available and make some noise for your pal Sals. Tell the online world about your primo and the book I worked very diligently on.

Don't forget to follow me:

facebook.com/PalsOfSals/

yourpalsals on IG

yourpalsals on Twitter

yourpalsals on Tic Tok

youtube.com/@yourpalsals

redbubble.com/people/yourpalsals